Break Loose. Enjoy Life!
The Missing Link to Happiness.

Channeled by Estella

Copyright © 2015 Fay Rayner

All rights are reserved. The material contained within this book is protected by copyright law. No part may be copied, reproduced, presented, stored, communicated or transmitted in any form by any means without prior written permission. Enquiries should be made to the publisher at www.EstellasMessages.com

Author: Estella
Title: Break Loose. Enjoy Life! The Missing Link To Happiness.
Edition: First edition.

ISBN: 978-0-646-93705-2

Notes: Includes Table of Contents

Subjects: Self Help
            Spirituality
            New Age

Cover Image © Copyright Fay Rayner
Cover design: www.HubsiteBuilder.com.au

Publisher: Fay Rayner, Australia
Website: www.EstellasMessages.com
Email: estella@estellasmessages.com

Contents

Break Loose. Enjoy Life! 1
   FREE DOWNLOAD 4
   Introduction to the Masters 5
      Mother Mary 5
      Osiris 5
      Thoth 5
      Sananda 6
      Abraham 6
   Messages from the Masters 7
      Thoth: Don't let fear control your life 7
      Mother Mary: Challenges come to strengthen you 10
      Osiris: Learn to enjoy your life 13
      Mother Mary: Do you ever think of yourself? 16
      Thoth: A relaxing meditation 20
      Osiris: Don't be afraid to open your heart 22
      Osiris: You're an amazing being. Learn about yourself! 24
      Sananda: Do you fully realise the strength you already have? 27
      Mother Mary: What would you really like to do with your life? .. 31
      Abraham: Believe in yourself and know what you want 37
      Thoth: Be your own person 40
      Osiris: How to have a happy and enjoyable life 43

Mother Mary: What would you really like to do with your life?.. 45
Osiris: It's your choice to be loved or unloved 48
Mother Mary: Clear your mind and your body 52
Thoth: The past does not have to affect your future 55

FREE DOWNLOAD

Download a lovely relaxation audio,
channeled by Estella.
Go to www.EstellasMessages.com

Introduction to the Masters

Do you ever wonder what life is all about? How some people have such a happy life and others struggle and nothing is pleasant about their life?

Well I hope the messages from these great Masters will help you change your life to happiness.

Mother Mary
Mother Mary is the mother of Jesus of Nazareth in Christian and Islamic scriptures. Catholicism and some other Christian traditions honour her as a special saint, the "blessed virgin," who hears and acts upon prayers. She was a child of the Essene and when they did something that was not quite right, they were supported to understand the experience rather than be punished for it

Osiris
Osiris as well as being a god of the dead, Osiris was a god of resurrection and fertility. In fact, the ancient Egyptians believed that Osiris gave them the gift of barley, one of their most important crops.

Thoth
Thoth, known in Egyptian myths as the great record keeper, was associated with the arbitration of godly disputes, the arts of magic, the system of writing, the development of science, and the judgment of the dead.

Sananda
The Ascended Master Sananda / Jesus / Christ serves as the World Teacher and was one of the great Spiritual Healers who walked our beloved planet Earth. He works with Archangel Uriel to bring peace, brotherhood, service and freedom to people

Abraham
Our forefather, Abraham, not only taught the world about God; he taught us how to discover Him. Abraham delivers a message of joy and creation through dialogue with a group of spiritually evolved teachers who call themselves Abraham.

Love,
Estella

Messages from the Masters

Thoth: Don't let fear control your life

We'd love to help with your book because so many people are down in the dumps; they don't realise they can lift themselves up, and feel good. So I'd be pleased to help you.

Help them now. Yes, it is I, Thoth. What I would like to put into a book is the fact that everybody who has come into this life has come to learn lessons, to enjoy themselves, to enjoy and have fun. But the thing is, fear has caught up with so many people, they fear everything - fear that someone is going to hurt them, fear that someone is going to take their job, everywhere they look it's fearful.

We must explain that we need to get off this fear, and people say "it's alright for you to say this but we're in the predicament, we are in the mess that we are, how can we possibly say this is great, that we're having a good time, when we're really not? When we're having a really hard time it's really hard."

Well, the thing is. you need to break the cycle that you're in, break that cycle, just give it a go even though you think it's not really going to work, at least try and give it a go - maybe on the weekend, just try in the morning as soon as you wake up, think what a beautiful day it is.
If you had a good sleep, then remember to say "Oh thanks for this great sleep I just had!" And if you haven't, well, don't dwell on that, think of

positive things - you've got a roof over your head; you may be in debt, but at this moment have you got a roof over your head? Be thankful; some people don't. Is the air outside nice? Are there trees out there you can look at?

Think of all the nice things and even if you go for an hour you are breaking the cycle and just feel the difference.

If you work on it, thinking of no problems for an hour - that's not really asking much. You get up thinking of all pleasant things and just feel how you're going and if you're feeling OK try to go a little bit further.

If the children are screaming don't start yelling, don't start yelling. Think of something nice to say. You know what, when you are calm and feeling positive you'll be amazed at the difference on the children as well, because they pick up on your vibration when you're yelling or cranky or upset or tearful. They feel those feelings so they get upset too, then they start mucking up and it's a vicious circle.

So if you're starting the day feeling good for that hour, then you've got till the next hour to just take notice of what your family are doing. It is more peaceful and the day is calmer.

So you've done a test run and you can see how it works, now you can continue, whether it's for work or whatever. Endeavour to think positive even when you think there's nothing positive about this, just think, in that day, can I think of something, can I think of something that's nice even if it's just the sky looks beautiful or that flower is gorgeous.

Get yourself into the positive, get yourself thinking happy. When you think happy your day will be happy. Give it a go. You may be surprised; you really may be surprised. Once you start breaking that circle of negativity and fear you will be amazed at how your life will change.

I'm hoping you will give it a go and I'm sending you my love,
Thoth

Mother Mary: Challenges come to strengthen you

I would love to say things are much better than people realise.

Their life has many challenges, but you know those challenges help strengthen them, the challenges are there to strengthen them, the challenges are there to strengthen them and then think back at how they worked through them and that they did work through them.

When that challenge first started they thought they would never get through it. They thought it was just too difficult, but when they look back they can see that they have coped, they have survived. They still have food on the table; they have a roof over their head.

There are still many challenges to come but as Thoth said, 'must get the positivity going' and although many people they will reject that idea and not attempt it they will find it hard to get out of the situation they are in, but if you at least try, do the thinking positive, see love, feel love and be happy, smile, laugh, laugh at yourself.

You know sometimes you can do something then think "how on earth did I do that?" Or you can put something down and you can't find it, you can look round and round and you can't find it and there its staring you straight in the face! Laugh about it, don't get cranky about it - laugh! Laughing gets the fear out of you; laughing gets the anger out; laughing gets the happiness into you and once you start to get happy, things change and you feel so much better.

So think of these things: happiness, laughing, seeing nice things where normally you would look and say, "Oh, that is shocking!" Look at it again and find something that is nice, find something that will cheer you up.

Have you ever done something and it really gives you a good kick, really makes you feel great? When you feel down in the dumps and when you look around and there is absolutely nothing I can think of that is nice, can't see a thing, think of that thing that made you really happy.

It can be something you did years ago, or it could have been something you did last week. Find something before you start doing your positivity. Find something that always makes you feel happy. You might have seen someone do something funny, or something that a child has done that you thought how clever, that's really lovely, just find something that you have done that always makes you feel happy when you think about it, so that when you're down in the dumps think of that, go back to that, if you can't think of anything else, go back to that if it makes you cheerful.

Once you break that cycle, once you break that cycle of feeling down in the dumps, things can change, but they can't change if you're spiraling down; you've got to stop and pick yourself up.

So think of that funny thing that really cheers you up or that lovely thing that cheers you up and then once you've broken that spiral you've got a chance to see something nice about what you're doing. Always find something nice even if someone is really cranky at you, really nasty; pull back before you answer, look at them while they are doing it and find something that is humorous about the way they are going on.

Don't feed them, don't feed them - that's what they want; they are getting cranky and maybe yelling at you. They want you to yell back - don't! Don't feed their anger. Pull back, pull back.

There is so much in this life, there is so much happiness there, there is so much love there for you, and we want you to feel our love. We are with you all the time, we love you. So feel our love and feel yourself, feel yourself pulling yourself out of the doldrums, feel yourself getting happy and loving your life, because you're in that body for such a short time, so enjoy it, enjoy your life.

This is Mother Mary and I wish you well. I send you my love.
Good bye.

Osiris: Learn to enjoy your life

I am Osiris, and I come today to talk to you, to talk to you about things in the past that have happened. Terrible things that people would think the world would never be the same, but back in my day there were so many things happened that we would think the world had come to an end it has been so bad, then somehow the things change and things are rosy again and that is what we need to get you to remember - that ups and downs in life make it interesting.

When you are down it's not so interesting and you think you will never come up and when you are down there is only one way to go and that's up. So remember, whatever is happening you can't go further than down, you are going to start to come up. So wherever you are now, how about stopping there and getting on with life and coming up? Coming up to enjoy, coming up to be excited!

Each morning when you wake up, be excited the day has started, you're alive, and you're breathing.

As you've been told previously, think positive when you first wake up, that's the time to plan the day, to plan that you're going to have a great day, enjoy it.

Look at those people who have been in these camps and they have nothing, absolutely nothing! They have been tortured, all horrid things done to them, yet, at the end they have survived, because although they have gone through things that most people would not even think of, they kept positive, they kept thinking that right we've gotten through another day and the next day has to be better, and although they have gone through all this trauma, somehow they survived.

The people who didn't, the people who had exactly the same problems in these camps, who were down on themselves and thinking sorrowful things, they have died because they didn't have the positive thoughts to pull themselves up.

So that's what you all need my dears; you need to have the strength to keep the positivity, to use your brain - that's what you've got it for. You know the scientists say you've only used about 10 percent of your brain; that's because the rest of it is different to what they are expecting. It's the power of the brain; there is so much power there.

If you think positive, you think happy, that's what you're going to have, but it's not much use saying you tried being happy and it didn't work - maybe you were thinking in two thoughts - I'll try this but I know that it won't work. Naturally it won't work - you have to really want it to work. Even if it's only for 15 minutes and then expand on it. Remember these people who got through trauma and survived? They are the strong ones; not strong in body because lots of them were starved and whipped and worked so hard, yet they had the mental power to pull themselves through. And yet, as I said, people who had the exact same things happening to them fell by the way and died.

You don't want to be one of those people. You want to be one of the strong ones, the strong ones who can cope with everything and then start to see the light at the end of the tunnel as you say.

Those people can see that things are changing and are changing with them. People around them change also because you've got to remember you are energy, you are vibrational energy creatures, you give out an energy field, or what you call an aura and this aura touches other people. So if your aura is happy others that come into your path will start to change too. So you're not just changing yourself, you are changing others.

So think of it this way, think of it as your strength, your love, your happiness and pull that through to see a new you.

I hope this helped you. This is Osiris,
Good bye.

Mother Mary: Do you ever think of yourself?

Welcome sweeties, this is Mother Mary,

Have you ever thought of yourself? You know you rush around and work and do everything - have you ever thought of yourself?

When are you showing the real self? You are different things to different people. You are a friend, a mother or a father, a brother or a sister and you have to be different people to each one.

When you're talking to a sister or brother it's different to how you speak to a stranger. So you've got all these different people inside you, all struggling to do what they have to do, but have you ever thought about the real you?

Have you ever taken yourself to a quiet spot and just sat and relaxed and looked around you? You could be in a park near a river; you could be anywhere, just as long as you can find a spot that's quiet, just by yourself.

Just bring out the real you, how you really feel. You've got an inner self that really is the real you, the one that wants to be the strong one or wants to do different things.
You've also got the one that shows to the real world and that's completely different. Sometimes we want to put on a show that everything is alright, that we are happy, everything is going alright, but

then when we are by ourselves we are tearful, and wondering how are we going to keep going.

So while you're sitting there in this peaceful spot let's combine the two, bring that one that has the show and the one that's maybe a little like marshmallow together.

It's a little fragile and let's think of how we act when we are positive and putting on a show. When we are putting on a show that everything is alright we are showing there is a positivity coming out of us.

That positivity I want you to keep, sit there and think about it, think how you feel when you're the actor or actress, think how you feel. You feel more secure, you feel confident, and then you let yourself slide back into, what I call the marshmallow. You come back to this fragile person.

How about trying to keep that person who's on show, keep the positive, keep the showmanship, and you will find by keeping that showmanship that everything is all right - I'm strong, I can do this, and I can do anything.
If you can keep that up you will pull that marshmallow person up, you will pull that marshmallow person and strengthen them and you will become the person you are pretending to be.

Just pretend that you can do anything, you know you can, you have the power and the strength to do it, just keep being the showman of positiveness, the person that other people think, "Gee they can handle anything!" Be that person; truly be that person.

It's a simple enough thing to do - every time you're with people you become the showman, so just bring that showman back to yourself, and while you are sitting there in that peaceful place, just think of how you acted when you were with the last person you were with, how you pretended.

Think about it; doesn't it give you a bit of a giggle, a bit of a laugh that you were so strong, so able to cope with anything, and they didn't know how you really felt? Bring the two together, bring the two.

You know even having a little laugh at yourself is changing your energy field. You can laugh at what you've done; just give yourself a little laugh and that breaks the fear, it breaks the uncertainty. Have a laugh or even think of something funny that someone else did or you did.
Break the cycle, bring yourself out of fear. Bring yourself to happiness and love and as I said, laughing helps do that. You can just laugh, give yourself a bit of a laugh to break the negative, to break the fear and to get into happy mode.

Happiness and love will bring you everywhere, but you need to love yourself. To love yourself is the most important; don't feel selfish - yourself is important, very important. So love yourself! When you love yourself and you are happy with yourself, you can give happiness and love to other people. You have to love yourself because you are a wonderful person. Remember, you are a wonderful person.

This is Mother Mary.
Good bye.

Thoth: A relaxing meditation

I, Thoth, would like to take you on a beautiful, relaxing happy meditation.

Just see yourself; just see yourself as a bird, a beautiful bird, a bird that has beautiful colours in the feathers. Pick the colours that you suit, that you love and spread your wings, spread them and be caught up with the breeze.

Just feel yourself swirling around in the breeze, and as the breeze swirls around, you're going higher and higher. What a beautiful feeling, no cares and no problems, just the sheer delight of weightlessness.

You can't hear anything, just drifting, drifting, and drifting. Just your mind emptying out, there are no thoughts, you are just there, no thoughts, no worries, just being, just being in the moment, the moment you have feelings of just sheer joy, sheer joy as you just drift with the breeze.

Just feel, just feel how you feel; you have complete freedom, complete freedom and complete joy. And feel this freedom and joy as you drift back, as you drift back down, you can feel yourself coming back and as you come back, and as you come back, this feeling of joy and happiness, let it continue through your life feel the joy the freedom, the freedom of knowing that you can do whatever you like.

Clear your mind and just relax.

When you relax your energies just fly, they strengthen. Just relax and enjoy your day.

And this is Thoth saying,
Good bye.

Osiris: Don't be afraid to open your heart

I would like to talk to you this moment. The time is right to open the heart, to open the heart and let people get close.

Don't alienate people; bring closeness, because strength is when you're together, when you communicate, and at times things happen and by yourself it's hard to cope with, but when you get together there is a bond, there is a strength, and together it is much easier to get though troubled times.

People often think when they are a bit down or they have a problem that nobody else will understand, so they keep it all to themselves, but you know everyone has these times, so people do understand, but unless you're open and speak, you won't know that they understand and they won't know you need an ear to be listened to, to console.

Being a collective has always been the strength through the ages; no one by themselves can win a battle, but with togetherness you can, and that's the same if it's an emotional problem or a physical problem.

Strength is with those around you. Don't be frightened to open your heart; people can sit in a corner and get really upset and keep everything bottled up, and when you bottle up problems, it's like a big volcano waiting to bubble up and explode, and then it becomes such a big mess, such a big mess, and if it was let out earlier …

You can see where I'm going, that it would not be a big mess, it may be uncomfortable because sometimes when you're letting out the problem or the worry you have, you feel embarrassed, you worry about what other people are going to say. Will they think you're mad, silly or something? But you'll be amazed at the help you'll get.

So please remember, let people in even if at the time it seems impossible, open your mouth, open your mind, open your heart, and if you're the person who is listening, open your heart as well because no one knows from one day to another what is going to happen.

Today you might be perfectly healthy, everything going perfectly fine and you may just trip over and do quite a bit of damage to yourself. Or a car maybe might not see you; lots of things can happen that can put you in an awkward position, so have sympathy, have a nice ear and listen to the person and from your heart to their heart let them know that you are sending them love.

This is Osiris, till next time.
Goodbye.

Osiris: You're an amazing being. Learn about yourself!

I welcome you all, this is Osiris.

I welcome you to the fact that you want to understand more about yourself. You're an amazing being; you don't realise just how amazing you are and you use so little of the brain but don't even wonder what the other part is for. The other part is you controlling your life, the power of your brain of thought. Thought is just so important.

Whether you think nice things or negative things, they all affect the way your life travels, so wouldn't it be easier to have it going nicely, so you're putting all positive things out and although we know it's difficult because sometimes you're in such a problem situation, but it's worth giving it a go.

We've mentioned it before and you probably thought, "Oh not that again!" But really it is so important and that is why we keep repeating ourselves to get you to take the time to just think positive, just for even a short time, just test try it, just give it a go, just for a couple of hours, just thinking of nice things.

Don't bite your tongue and try and think nice things and then in the back of your mind think that this is just rubbish! Don't do that, because it won't work, it won't work. We want to see you feeling really great.

Now, now that you've started on your way to channeling your energies into nice things so that your life is going much better, just think of the different things that you could have.

You could have a better job or inner peace, which is always the best thing. If you've got inner peace, you feel great within yourself.

Now that you've picked yourself up a little bit, start channeling yourself into what you really want, things that you probably haven't told anybody about. Start thinking about those things, start imagining that you're doing them and you will see your life starting to curve in that direction because quite often you really would love to do something but you think, "Oh that's silly; I'm not going to tell anybody about that."

Well, we're not just anyone; we're here to help you and help guide you. We're here to assist you in any way we can, but, you've got freedom of will so you're the one that has to decide whether you really want to do something or not, so, even write it down, you don't have to show anyone.

Just write down what you would really, really like and be good with yourself, don't make it such a small thing, make it huge, just write down what you really want to do and then each morning and before you go to bed look at it and think about it and imagine you've actually got it, you've actually got it.

Make a game if you like; a game just you and your spirits or your subconscious, whatever you want to call us, you are playing a game with us, even date it, date it, because it's funny how when things change just gradually and gradually and gradually, at the end when you've got what you want, you can't remember how it all started. So you date this and each month just look at it and then see what's changed in your life.

You'll be amazed at things you've forgotten. It's like when you have a headache, you have a headache and then it goes and when you had the headache you felt so bad but when its gone you forget all about it and that's the same with things that are happening and changing in your life.

You want it but then as it changes you completely forget, oh that's what I really wanted and I wrote it down so many weeks or months ago - it's come true, it's really come true!

So you can actually track these things down. I hope this helps you, because that's all we want to do, when you are happy we get so excited because you don't realise that we see through your eyes; we're seeing the happiness, we're seeing you excited, then we get excited too. So we're on the journey with you, we're always with you, and we love, we just love when you're happy. Enjoy your new, you might say homework, your new passion, and we will talk to you again.

This is Osiris, till next time.
Goodbye.

Sananda: Do you fully realise the strength you already have?

I, Sananda, am so pleased to talk to you. It is a great honour to speak to you.

Let's go inside your head. How does it feel? Does it feel sure of itself? Just sit for a moment, just take a few minutes for yourself, just feel how your head feels. You know, you've got so much strength and knowledge in that brain of yours that you don't realise.

Have you ever sat down in meditation? You may never have meditated before, so just sit down and relax and just blot out the rest of the world for a short time and go into your imagination, see what you like to do.

Do you like to bush walk? Do you like to ride motor bikes? Do you like to go to the circus? Just think of these things because in your mind you can do anything you want, anything, and it's so beautiful just to sit down and go inside and imagine all those things, because your life that you call a real life is a dream anyway, so why not do a dream that you really want to do, and have it turn out the way you want it to?

You might have a dream about a life that you would like to have, things that you have wanted for a long time, just take a few minutes and think of what you would love to do. If it's just having fun or changing your life, whatever it is, just forget about everything else, and just have that ride through your imagination, I'm going to leave you for a few minutes so you can do it.

....

Now, we are only going to have a short time this time, but the thing is you can do this later and take as long as you like and just in that short time, just see how you feel ... do you feel calmer and just more relaxed?

And that's because you've forgotten about the tension of the day, you've let it go for a few minutes. Doesn't it feel good just to feel peaceful for a change?

Now remember, you can do this at any time and I know people will say I haven't got enough time but, you know, actually, in the universe there is no time, so you can make the time that you want.

Say you have to catch a train by a certain time, just set it, well I'm going to be catching that train and I'm going to be there well and truly before it comes, or I have an appointment and I'll be there well and truly beforehand. Don't rush you'll be amazed that because you've set the time and said that you'll be there before that particular time and trust it, you'll be there at that time!
So you can say, "In the morning I'm going to have at least 15 minutes to sit quietly with no interruption so I can sit and start the day off without any interruption, so I can be at peace with myself." Because, if you start the day off feeling peaceful, then you'll find the whole day goes well, so by doing this you can sit down and go into your day dreams, you can go

into whatever you wanted to do and how you wanted to become a great actress or you wanted to be a great singer, in your dreams you can do that.

You can be the best tennis player. You can be whatever you like. So you can give yourself those 15 minutes in the morning just so you can have your own time.

You might tell yourself that you've got children and they are always at you, but just try saying at this particular time of the day, "I'm going to have me time and no one will interrupt me." You will find the children are watching television, or getting dressed; they are doing other things, and you'll be amazed that they won't interrupt you, so give it a go.

As I said, there are so many things that you can dream that you can do, just go with it, just go with the flow, just think beautiful things and feel the inner peace that you have at the end and it's all just because you've blotted out the day that you've thought you were going to have, worrying about it, worrying about the children or worrying about friends; all of that is gone just for that short time, and that short time it's going to affect your whole day.

I hope this helps you feel really good and you have a really good day, because that's what we are here for; we are here to learn and have fun and what better way than to feel at peace within yourself.

Thank you for listening to me.

This is Sananda.
Goodbye

Mother Mary: What would you really like to do with your life?

Welcome dear ones, welcome to another chat.

It's interesting all the different things we can talk about and you know it all boils down to de-stressing you, keeping you relaxed and for you to use the strength of your mind; to use the strength of your mind in what you're doing and they are the two main things whichever way we talk about things that's what it comes back to.

We need to work out ways to keep calm and have that inner peace and we need to decide our path, set our goals and use the power of your mind to do just that.

Now, a lot of people say that" I don't have a clue what I want to do, I'm not happy with what I'm doing, but I don't know which way to go." So, how about tonight or today, whichever time it is that you are listening to our talk?

You sit down and I'm going to send a beautiful golden ball of light going right over you, just relax, and just see yourself being calm.

Just have a nice, deep breath, in and out; just relax, just let everything drift from your mind, and just feel the beautiful golden light coming down through your head and into your chakras, coming right through your body, right through to your toes.

You can feel the tingling and then feel it spreading right through your body, out into your auric field, and now you're in a big egg shape of golden light. Just get the feel of it first before we go any further.

Now, how are you feeling? Are you feeling relaxed, are you feeling calm?

What we are going to do is just to let you drift back, just drift back in time, just drift back till you were a baby, drift back, just drift back to when you were in the womb, just feel yourself drifting away, just drifting back.

Now we are going to drift back further, we are going to drift back to before you planned to come into this life. See your circle of family sitting around you and just listen to all the chatter, all the chatter about what you want to do and how they are going to help you, how they are going to guide you.

I want to take time to really go deep, go deep within yourself, and just listen to a few of the ideas you were going to do before you came in, the things that you had planned; they can change of course, but just take time just to listen to all the chatter and to all the thoughts of what you had intended to do.

By listening it just may give you an inkling of an idea of where you wanted to go or what you wanted to do, just to give you an idea of the path you were thinking of before you came in, this may help you.

So I am going to leave you now for a while, so you can just listen and you can have a chat too; you're back there with the group, so give your ideas and listen to theirs and see what comes of it. We'll talk soon.

Ask those around you how they are going to help you, because they know that when you come into this earthly body that you have free will, so they can't make you do anything; they can only help you.

Ask them how they are going to do that; how they are going to help you stay on the path that you planned to come on. And have you any ideas now of the path you wanted to follow? Now, thank them for their guidance, then, let them know you will appreciate them helping you, although, once you are in your earthly body you won't realise it, but let them know ahead of time you will appreciate their guidance.

Now, just slowly roll back, just come back, just come back and as you're coming back stop anywhere that you feel that time in your life changed the direction you were going in. It may have been when you were very young, or it may have been when you were a teenager, something happen in your life, just let yourself drift back until you can come to a time that's changed your ideas.

Think about that time, and take a good look at it and see why you think it changed your ideas. Did it change your ideas for the good or not? What lesson did you learn from that situation? Just let your mind drift over the situation and see what you learnt from it.

Now, understanding that situation will be interesting to see how it changes your thoughts, but for now let's just drift back, drift back to being back in that beautiful golden egg of energy.

Just think about the things you've just gone through and just see if it helps you understand the path that you need to take. Are you already on that path? Or do you need to make a few changes?

If you're already on that path, think about ways you can strengthen it and widen the path, be more involved in the plan you have.

If you've side tracked it a little bit, think about ways you can change to make yourself feel happier and more accomplished.

Quite often, it doesn't take very much; you need to change just a few things. Usually it's your thought patterns, getting yourself feeling positive and confident. Quiet often we allow ourselves to become unconfident in ourselves.

Quiet often we let people see a different person to who we really are, so you've got two people in you, really three people, the real you, the person you think you are and the person who other people think you are.

Just see if you can make a few changes about bringing yourself into balance. Because when you are in balance, when you're showing to others the same as how you feel and what you really are, you're the real you and you're a happier you, more positive and able to handle anything that comes your way.

Just think about yourself and which situation you are in and how, with small changes, you can bring yourself into complete balance. With the energy around you, it will help bring out the positive and the confidence in you, because that golden light around you knows you and the real you will start to come through and start to help you.

Just feel the confidence in yourself in the path you are happy to take. Just take the time to feel this. Feel this beautiful energy coming right through you, through every cell in your body, through your emotions; just feel it flow through you.

Now that you're coming into balance, you're going to feel so much better, so much happier in yourself, because when you're balanced there's just a beautiful warm feeling that's in you and it's a feeling that you can just do anything, you can accomplish anything, and that's the real you coming through.

It's amazing how confidence and bringing balance changes your thoughts, because now you know you can do whatever you want, you can accomplish anything; it's just a matter of setting a goal, setting your mind right onto it and doing it.

We know it sounds easy and we know that you need to work on it, but the thing is that we are here to help you at all times, so when it does become a little difficult, just call on us and we are there to help you.

Your guardian angel is always there to help you, your higher self you can always talk to, there are so many you can talk to and want to talk to you.

You've got plenty of assistance, but unless you talk to us and ask, we can't help you as much as we would like because we just want so much to help with all your situations; we just want to help.

I hope this has bought different thoughts into your mind and I hope that this has helped you a little.

We've enjoyed talking to you.
Until next time,
Goodbye.

Abraham: Believe in yourself and know what you want

Welcome, I am here to discuss what you would like to know.

You know I've always been one for teaching positivity like all my other friends, but with a bit of a twist, remembering that you can have whatever you like - businesses, money, whatever, but you need to stay positive and believe in yourself and you know that half the battle is believing in yourself, trusting yourself.

So many people just swing with whatever other people say. They want to be one of the group, they want to be popular, so whatever the group wants, that's what you want, but you know that's not how you succeed. You succeed by being your own person, trusting in yourself and knowing what you want.

Knowing what you want is the important thing, because when people want something and they think maybe that's too hard for them or maybe they're not good enough for that. Well obviously you're not going to get it, but when you think of something that you really want and you go for it, you believe it, you feel it, then it's going to come true.

Your emotions are very, very important because how you feel is the thing, how you really feel. If you feel really good about something, well, you're on the right track. When you want something, but you feel nervous and not so happy about it, you need to think about why you really want it. It's probably something someone else has suggested that would be good to have and not something that you really have thought about.

The way to know if something is right for you is how you feel. If you're feeling really good and happy and excited, you know that's the path for you, and then think about it and dream about it, really get excited about it. It hasn't got to be just some small thing, enlarge it, and see it bigger, bigger than ever.

To get excited about what you're doing is half the battle, you're there, because all the negative stuff is gone, you've all got the positive, you're feeling good in yourself and that's what we want to see, we want to see you feeling happy and feeling really great in yourself, that's the whole reason you came down into this body; to have fun and to learn, not to be scared and upset and worried all the time. That's not the way to go, it is definitely not the way to go.

So keep the positivity, keep being excited about what you want, because the minute you're not excited about it, think about it, you've gone off the track a bit and come back, that's what's gone wrong here, why are we not so happy.
You probably just strayed a little bit, so then work on it and come back to where you were happy. It's like a radio station - you move the dial and it blurts out horrible noises and then you go a little bit further and you get it spot on, but if you're just off the channel, it's all blurred and horrible noises, and that's the same with yourself.

When you're on the path you feel great and when you're not on the path, you don't feel good, so the thing is to feel good, get back on that path, see what has happened and climb back on it again.

I've enjoyed this time with you.

This is Abraham, thank you.
Goodbye.

Thoth: Be your own person

I, Thoth, have been writing for centuries and helping people write. The thing is to just feel and know that what you're writing is going to help people.

Tonight, let's talk about how people interact with other people.

Quite often you notice that someone will suggest something and the other person will say that's not right and try and force their opinion on them. You know everyone has the right to their opinion and when you disagree with someone, don't worry about it, it's their opinion and they want to do it. Unless it involves you directly agree to disagree. Say, "I appreciate that is your opinion, mine is a little bit different, but you're best to go with what you feel is right for you."

Don't force your opinion on someone else; you have no right to do that. You and your body and your mind are all your concern, no one else's. So think about yourself. Quite often people have enough things to think about of their own without worrying about trying to organise someone else. Think about the things you need to do, think about the things you're trying to solve. Sit down and think about it. Sometimes you get so uptight about things, you have so much to do and you don't get anything done and you seem to go around in circles.

Have you thought about writing down what you need to do? It seems to take a load off your mind by writing it down, and by writing it down you can look at it and say, "Right, this is the most important thing."

Number them and do them in order and don't get distracted. Don't start half way through and then jump to something else; stick to what you have said is the one you are going to do now, the most important and then the next one. When done, cross it off and you'll feel so accomplished because you'll get so much more done by doing it this way.

What you don't get done obviously wasn't important enough, so put it on the list for the next day, put it first on your list for the next day or in order of importance, but make a list so that you're not jumping around, because that's what gets you all uptight. You don't seem to get anywhere; you don't get anything done because you're jumping around.

Write them as soon as you wake up, give thanks for the day, give thanks that you're alive, that it's a beautiful day out there; it may be raining but still the plants will be really happy.

Give thanks for things that you know that you're so fortunate to have - a roof over your head, a nice family, clothes to wear, what is important to you, give thanks for that before you start.

Be thankful that you have good health, or if you're improving, your health your getting much better every day, then write down your list for the day, so you know precisely what you're doing and as we said, stick to it. You'll get so much more done this way, so much more, and when you think about it, you think oh that's a silly idea, just really think about your day, do you jump all over the place and find that you're not getting anything done?

So try this method and see if you're more accomplished by doing this. It's worth a try isn't it? Then, by getting it done quicker, getting through all the things you'll have more time to relax, maybe read a book, go for a walk.

But you've got time for you and it is so important to have you time, it really is; just to sit down and do whatever you really want. You might want to do a bit of gardening, or just sit down and listen to the birds, smell the scent of the flowers, or feel the breeze in your hair, just to do absolutely nothing is always a good one too.

But do it! You've got the time now because you've organised yourself. You'll feel so much better. I hope this helps you.

This is Thoth, till next time,
Goodbye.

Osiris: How to have a happy and enjoyable life

I am Osiris and I'm here to give you some more information; information on how to have a happy enjoyable life; one where you are proud of yourself.

Now you'll probably say that's impossible! It isn't, it never is, it's all up to you remembering or you might not realise what you think about is what happens and again you might say, "I haven't thought about all these things that are happening to me." But you know you have.

Humans these days or anytime really, are thinking all the time, all the time, they'll think of something that's really, really good, but they back track and say something bad, and they wonder why things happen. It's because you're thinking things and not thinking it through.

Start to think and know what you're thinking, think things that you would like to happen. Think things that would make you happy. Don't be all over the shop, don't be thinking this and that, and I wish I had money, I haven't got any money, I need this, I need that. Stop doing that, stop it!

Concentrate and think about what's going into your mind. What you think is the most important thing. People think what they say is, People say one thing and they think something completely different. It's what you think that's important.

So start thinking about what you think. Think positively. Don't think positively and then backtrack. Don't say, "I will have that' and then think to yourself, "That's too good for me. I'll never get that." It's not the way to do it. Keep on the positive, keep on the happy.

When you're happy and laughing, your energies are working for you, but when you start getting in the crankiness and down in the dumps everything is going against you and you know that because everything just goes bad.

You know that when you are miserable and you're feeling miserable and you are miserable, but you know that, change it. Remember how we previously said to have something that really makes you happy, have something that really makes you really happy so that when you're in the doldrums like that, you can pull back and think of the thing that makes you happy, gets you out of the doldrums, gets you into the happy mode again, thinking nice, looking around, seeing how lucky you are.

I know I seem to be pushing all the time but all I want for you is that you'll be happy and enjoy your life. If I have to be pushy to do it I will, because for so long you've just thought these negative things and wondered why things aren't going right.

Start being happy, enjoy your life. Enjoy this life.

Goodbye.
Osiris

Mother Mary: What would you really like to do with your life?

Welcome dear ones, this is Mother Mary.

You came into this life to enjoy, to learn, and to be so happy, but so many of you feel that you have to make other people happy. You have to make the boss happy, your family happy, and your friends happy, you feel that you need to bend to what they want.

Now, the main thing is to make you happy. A lot of you find you are not confident to do this, you feel your strength is doing what these other people expect of you.

But you know you can make yourself happy, you can build your confidence up. The main thing is what you would like to do. What would you really like to do?

If you were on an island with no one around and anything you want to do you could do, think of what you would really like to do. There's no one else to worry about. No one to answer to. Think of what you would really like to do.

Now, give it a go, even if it's a couple of hours, doing something that you would really like to do. You feel good in yourself, you feel confident. It's amazing how happy you feel when you do something you really want to do and you're not worrying about anybody else. You know if you keep doing this from hour to hour, doing things the way you would like to do, you'll be amazed how it affects other people.

You know how you can walk into a room and everyone's arguing, you feel the tension, or if you go somewhere and everyone's happy, then it feels so wonderful. Well that's how you will affect other people. If you think about what you really want to do and do it. Sure you have to work, you have responsibilities, but when you do work, think of it in a positive way and enjoy doing it.

You say I don't like this work and you can't move on, there is no other job you can get. I'm sure you could really think about it and there'd be another way of doing something you really like. But if you can't and you're stuck in that situation, think of things that are nice, that you've been able to get to work, that you're healthy, you've got other people there that you can talk to, and you're earning money to buy things that you need.

Think of things that really make you happy and you know by doing this it's amazing how, when you're concentrating on making yourself happy, things will change; even if you're in that same job and maybe the people weren't as friendly as you like, be positive and happy within yourself.
It's amazing how the energy you give off will change those people; just gradually things will change and you'll be amazed, but the thing is that you have to try it , you have to do it to see it happen.

Keep yourself happy and be confident within yourself. Don't let other people run your life - you run your life. You're the most important person. Think happy thoughts and when you feel down, everyone gets down a little bit at times, think of things that make you happy and go and do things that make you happy, even if it's going for a bush walk, or going for a swim, doing something that brings you out of your doldrums and you'll be back being happy again.

There are so many things and so many reasons to be happy. You are living in such a beautiful time and a beautiful place. Give thanks; give thanks for everything you have, give thanks for being you, because you are a very special person.

Till next time, this is Mother Mary.

Osiris: It's your choice to be loved or unloved

Welcome to all. This is Osiris.

I want to talk about the choices we all make. There are so many choices; you can go along calmly or you can feel unloved, you can feel loved, you can feel unwanted; there are so many ways you can feel.

You can blame your family for everything that's happening to you, you can blame your situation on the government, and there are so many things you can blame. But you know when it all boils down that it's all up to you.

You're the one who has the say about what you do; your brain is so powerful you don't give it credit. People feel unwanted and then they start having drugs. The drugs don't give you love. Drugs just make you get down further.

Sure they help you feel alright for a short time, but not very long, so remember when you start taking these drugs, you're giving yourself to someone else, you've lost control of yourself, most probably what you want when you really think about it what you want is happiness and love and the drugs will not give you that.

The drugs will lower you further and as I say you're just giving yourself to someone else. Someone else is happy that you're buying the drugs because you have to pay them, and that makes them really happy because they've got that extra money.

Sometimes you have to do some quite not nice things to get the money, and so your life was started off as such a beautiful young child has changed. Whatever your circumstances, you still have the right to pull yourself up and have a good time, a good life.

You see some people who have everything, yet they're not happy and other people who have nothing and yet are happy. It's all in the strength of their minds.

So how about you showing the strength that you have? Go deep inside of yourself and find that strength. Give yourself to you, not to someone else. Love yourself, as we've said before, you're the most important person, so love yourself, feel happy within yourself, don't worry about other people, don't let other people influence you. Love yourself and think of what you really want to do.

Your brain is so powerful, but unfortunately most people don't give their brain credit. They just go from one thing they're thinking of to another, sometimes its positive and sometimes its quite negative, so they just bumble along from one day to another.

But if you sit down and think and plan what you would like to do, plan what you would really, really like to do and keep thinking of it, keep thinking of it, your life will be completely different.

Keep thinking of what you really want, how you would like to live your life and you will be amazed if you keep the thought up, but if you think about what you want and say oh I would love this you know it won't happen, keep that part out of it because then it won't happen.

It's like someone who's sick and they say, "I'll never get better." They won't get better because they don't believe they will, and that's the same with you.

Plan what you would like to do, how your life would make you happy and how you would like it to be, no matter what it is you're doing just keep this thought in your mind, keep it strong in your mind, and when you lay in bed see yourself, dream about it, see yourself doing it, keep it up, don't change it, keep it up, be strong with it and you will be amazed.

Document it when you start, document now what is happening and all about it, and then write down and date it and write down what you would really like to do.

You might want a different profession - it doesn't matter. Write down what you want, what you would like your life to be like and each month have a look and see the changes.

Write down the changes; they might be small to start with because maybe you haven't been really confident in your thoughts, but as each month goes you'll look back and think "My life really has changed."

How about giving it a go? Give it a go and see your life change.

Our main goal is to see you happy and we see you advancing and feeling good in yourself so let's be happy together, seeing you advance to what you really want.

This is Osiris and I bid you farewell for the moment.

Mother Mary: Clear your mind and your body

Good evening, I am so happy to be back to talk to you.

We talked about being positive; we've talked about concentrating on what we would really like to do.

Now we have our mind working let's get our body working.

To be able to function properly, we need our mind clear and we also need our body clear. We need to detox our body and the way to do that is to put aside the sugar.

We know you love the sugar, but you don't realise the damage it does to your body. You don't realise how much you take, a bottle of soft drink is so full of sugar, and everything that you pretty well touch in the shop for takeaway has lots of sugar in it.

So think of things, I know you like sweet things, so how about turning to fruit; fruit is nice and sweet, but your body can cope with that better.

Something that a lot of you treat as poison is water. Water flushes your system, it cleans you out. It's really very important to make sure you have five or six glasses of water a day. That doesn't mean water with coffee in it or water with juice in it, it means plain water.

Now so many people don't like to mention their bowels, but your bowel has to work properly to get rid of all the toxins out of your body and if it doesn't work properly, your skin tries to, but sometimes it's just overwhelmed. Look at your skin; is it pimply or uneven? Well then, think about your bowel.

Do you go to the toilet and use your bowel at least once a day? You know your body isn't a storage tank, and I know that a lot of people think that if they go once every couple of days that's fine, but when you put food into your body, you need to get rid of some.

Now, think about how your bowel works. If you're having trouble, a simple thing that you can help yourself is just before you go to bed have a glass of hot water, not from the hot water tap, but from the kettle, and before you have breakfast do the same thing, have a cup of hot water. This is like cleaning your system out before you start and you'll be amazed about how much better you feel if your bowel is working well.

Now, if we get that going and you're having your water and you've lain off the sugar, I think you'll find that you're feeling a lot better. You might think that this is going to be so hard, but it's amazing when you go off sugar for a couple of days.

Those couple of days may be hard but after that you don't really want it. I know it's hard to believe, but that's a fact, because your body is getting used to having the fruit and vegetables and your meat or chicken or whatever other protein that you like to have. Now, we're cleaning out your body and your body is getting healthier and I'm sure with doing all this you will find that you feel so much better.

One little extra thing is exercise. All you have to do is a brisk walk for about 30 minutes each day, and if you say you don't have time, well, how about getting up about 45 minutes earlier and getting ready and then going? You'll be amazed at how beautiful the air is early in the morning; it's just so fresh, just makes you feel so good.

Trying these few little adjustments to your diet and your physical being, within a couple of weeks you're not going to know yourself. I bet you even lose some weight and look so much better in your clothes. It's not hard to do, give it a go! Trust me, you will feel so much better.

We'll talk to this new person shortly, the new person who is going to be so healthy and that's you!

Till next time, goodbye.
Mother Mary

Thoth: The past does not have to affect your future

Estella: Good morning Thoth. It's a pleasure to have you with me this morning. What information will you give to help those people who doubt themselves and they just need help to get their life on track and feel great about themselves? What things can you tell us that are different from what we've been doing?

I am Thoth and I love to help people and I love to help you with your book. People now, I think if they're following us, have cleared their minds and are thinking positively and they are eating properly and now exercising however little it is, at least they're doing it. So now we need to get into deeper things.

A lot of people think that things in their past keep coming and mucking up their future, they say, "This always happens; it's just something that always happens. I go good for a little while and then I go down the drain."

But this doesn't have to be so; some people will say that they were given away at birth so they're unwanted, but that doesn't matter, all of you came into this life, and there are so many spirits wanting to come into these bodies and you did, they haven't, so whatever your circumstances are doesn't matter, it's all up to you. It's up to you what you want to make of your life.

We've gone through a lot already, so go back over the information and then come forward and start to plan like we did before for what you really want to do in your life.

Now if you've been following us, things should have changed and you should have noticed little things, even big things, especially if you wrote things down that have changed, you wrote down how you felt at the beginning and then each week or each month wrote down the changes you were experiencing.

Some people want money, but the thing is, if you just keep asking for money and then think, "I haven't got it" well, as you know from previous chapters, that's wasted effort. So think of what you want to do with the money and put that into your mind each morning and night or during the day that you're thinking about.

You might want to do a course, so instead of putting the money in your mind start thinking, " I would love to do a so and so course because it will help me develop my intuition, it will help me develop myself so I can help other people." Whatever the money is that you need, put in your mind what you need it for, forget about the money, just forget about the money, just put in your mind and keep it there and see it all the time what you want to do with the money. See yourself doing what you wanted.

It's the same with illness; people get sick and when someone asks how they are and they say "Oh, I feel terrible, I feel so terrible. No one can fix me!"

With that attitude, no one will be able to heal them, but, if you're ill, each day think, "Tomorrow I am going to be much better!" and keep that in your mind and when someone comes to say hello and ask how are you feeling, don't say you feel terrible. Instead, tell them that you're getting there; you're improving day by day. And keep that in your mind.

Some people will say "I'm sick and I feel terrible, so I can't say that!" Well, I'm sorry to say that's how you're going to stay, because you need to change your energies, you need to change your thoughts. It all sounds too hard, because crossing a huge mountain is hard, but crossing a little hill isn't.

So think of it in small amounts; don't try and win everything in a day. Think of what you want to buy, keep it in your mind and see yourself with it. It doesn't have to be small; it can be quite big.

Just say you want to own a huge factory, you need to concentrate and see yourself in that position. Dream of it, be with the thought, see yourself there and you will be amazed at the different things that come your way to help you on your way.

Because you can't fly a jet plane if you've never been in a jet or if you've never been taught, you have to learn on the way, but keep positive and know that each step that you do, you are learning and getting to the final thing you want.

There are so many things, anything you want is there, anything, but people don't realise this, anything you want is there, it's all just sitting there waiting for you to ask for it, but unfortunately you dear people ask for something and then back track, and it's in the back tracking that pulls you back, the doubting yourself.

You must start to get confident within yourself. Be confident that you are a special person, confident that you can do anything; it's just a matter of practising and you are doing it.

You know when you were a baby and you couldn't walk? Have you ever watched babies? They try so hard, they get up and fall over, they get up they fall over, they do it so many times, but they are determined they are going to walk and they do.

The same as when you go to school, your parents think, "How are they ever going to learn all they've got to learn to get ahead at school?"

Day by day, it doesn't take very long and these little kindergarten children are reading books and they are adding up; it's a day by day process. They are getting further and further advanced till they are mature adults, going out into the workforce.

Everything is step by step; put the major thought in your mind and keep it there. Stop going backwards and doubting yourself, because you are such great, great people.

You don't realise how great you are, how special you are. So please keep thinking and think positively.

This is me for today. Till next time, goodbye.
Thoth

....

My Notes:

www.ingramcontent.com/pod-product-compliance
Lightning Source LLC
Chambersburg PA
CBHW051710090426
42736CB00013B/2631